MAY 1 9 2002

J 979.40
Williams

The Essel
Californ.
c2003.

WITHDRAWN

The Library of
NATIVE AMERICANS

The Esselen
of California

Jack S. Williams

The Rosen Publishing Group's
PowerKids Press™
New York

For Bernard Fontana, who taught me that the most important thing that I could discover about people from other cultures was our common humanity

Published in 2003 by The Rosen Publishing Group, Inc.
29 East 21st Street, New York, NY 10010

Copyright © 2003 by The Rosen Publishing Group, Inc.

All rights reserved. No part of this book may be reproduced in any form without permission in writing from the publisher, except by a reviewer.

Photo and Illustration Credits: Cover and pp. 14, 21 courtesy of Mission San Carlos Borromeo, photos by Jack Williams; pp. 6, 16, 19 Jack Williams; p. 4 Erica Clendening; pp. 9, 23, 37, 45 courtesy of Mission San Carlos Borromeo, photos © Cristina Taccone; pp. 10, 12, 27 © Galen Rowell/CORBIS; p. 24 © Michael T. Sedam/CORBIS; pp. 29, 32 Museo Naval, Madrid (details from originals); pp. 40, 47 courtesy of the Bancroft Library, University of California, Berkeley; pp. 31, 53 Maria Melendez; p. 51 © CORBIS.

Book Design: Erica Clendening

Williams, Jack S.
  The Esselen of California / Jack S. Williams.
     p. cm. — (The library of Native Americans)
  Includes bibliographical references and index.
  Contents: Introducing the Esselen— Esselen technology—Other features of Esselen life—The Esselen and the newcomers (1542–1900)—The Esselen heritage.
  ISBN 0-8239-6433-7
  1. Esselen Indians—Juvenile literature. [1. Esselen Indians. 2. Indians of North America—California.] I. Title. II. Series.
  E99.E85 W55 2002
  979.4004'9757—dc21
                             2002002321

Manufactured in the United States of America

There are a variety of terminologies that have been employed when writing about Native Americans. There are sometimes differences between the original language used by a Native American group for certain names or vocabulary and the anglicized or modernized versions of such names or terms. Although this book contains terms that we feel will be most recognizable to our readership, there may also exist synonymous or native words that are preferred by certain speakers.

Contents

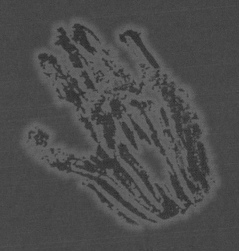

The Esselen and their Neighbors

Costanoan

Yokuts

Esselen

Salinan

Pacific Ocean

Area of Detail

California

Nevada

One

Introducing the Esselen

The morning fog and clouds often linger in the high mountain peaks along the beautiful rocky coastline that stretches south from Monterey, California. As the land slowly heats up, the clouds of mist sometimes swirl as they retreat in the direction of the ocean. Today, this land is the home of thousands of modern people who rarely take time to consider the past. Most know that Native Americans lived nearby at beautiful Mission San Carlos Borromeo. Few realize that many of the places that they see each day were once the homeland of another nation.

This book is about the Native Americans of this rugged mountain region. They are known today as the Esselen. They were never the largest or most powerful group to have lived in this part of North America. The records of their existence consist mostly of scattered objects that they left behind, such as arrowheads and seashells. A few descriptions written down by early settlers provide other clues about their way of life. By the time that their homeland became a part of the United States in 1848, independent Esselen communities could no longer be found. Their descendants had intermarried and combined with the other native groups that lived in the Monterey region.

This map depicts the region where the Esselen lived, in the areas south of present-day Monterey, California.

The Europeans invaded the Monterey region in 1770. When they began to colonize California, they were surprised that there were so many different native languages and customs. They recognized that the people who lived on the coast in Carmel and Monterey were different from the Native Americans who lived just to the south in the high mountains. The coastal groups to the west and north were usually described as Costeños by the Spaniards, and are now called Ohlones.

The grassy hills and oak forests of the eastern Esselen territory provided many useful sources of food and other resources.

The name Esselen is used to identify the mountain people who came from the village near where Mission San Carlos Borromeo was established. This place, which was probably located at the modern town of Carmel Valley, was called Eselenes, or Excelen. The name Eseleños, meaning people from the village of Eselenes, was slowly adopted by the Spaniards to describe all the mountain folk to the south of Mission San Carlos, and to the north of the territory of Mission San Antonio. San Antonio was founded for the Salinan Nation in 1771. Spaniards separated the Esselen from other groups because they spoke a different language. We do not know the name that the Esselen used to identify themselves.

The Esselen lands extended along the rocky California coast from Point Lopez to Big Sur, and into the interior to the Upper Carmel Valley and Junípero Serra Peak (elevation 5,844 feet, or 1,781m). The Esselen country measured about 580 square miles (1,502 square km). No one knows how many Esselen existed in 1770, but it seems likely that they numbered between five hundred and a thousand people based on the size of similar groups to the north and south.

No one knows when the Esselen first lived in this region. Most scholars believe that sometime between 13,000 and 40,000 years ago, people from Eastern Asia came to North America by crossing a frozen land bridge. These ancestors of the Native Americans slowly moved south. By 12,000 years ago, some of the groups had reached the southern tip of the Americas.

7

By about 8,000 years ago, some of these people had settled in the coastal areas of what would later be California. As time passed, many other nations moved into the same region, attracted by the abundant seafood that could be collected from the shoreline. In 1770, the Esselen represented the northern frontier of a series of major native groups that spoke a similar language, called Hokan by modern scholars. Beyond the Esselen area lived the Penutian-speaking coastal people who are called Ohlones.

Between 1770 and 1800, practically all the Esselen people moved into the mission at Carmel, which was known as San Carlos, or San Carlos Borromeo. During the period that followed, their numbers declined. Many of the surviving Esselen married Ohlones, who also lived at Mission Carmel.

Between 1835 and 1846, their most valuable traditional lands were taken over by Mexican ranch owners. After 1846, Native Americans all along the coast of California desperately tried to survive in the face of a century of discrimination and hatred. During the second half of the twentieth century, Esselen descendants established their place as representatives of an important, if little known, native nation.

In the pages that follow, you will get a chance to learn about some of the major events that took place among the Esselen since Europeans invaded their country in 1770. You will also read about some of the ways that the early Esselen lived. The fragments of evidence we have suggest that they shared many customs with their neighbors. Information drawn from our broader understanding of California Native Americans has been used to fill in some of the gaps in the Esselen story.

Most of the Esselen people made their home at Mission San Carlos Borromeo, also known as Mission Carmel, after 1770.

went without clothing. Throughout coastal California, the women usually wore more clothing than the men. Most adult females had two-piece skirts. When it was cold or wet, as it often was in the Esselen homeland, the people probably used blankets, robes, and capes. Like many other coastal groups, the men's hair was probably tied up in the back near the tops of their heads, or worn in braids. The women's hair probably fell down their shoulders and backs. The Esselen may have also worn hairnets. Both men and women probably wore jewelry, tattoos, and body paint.

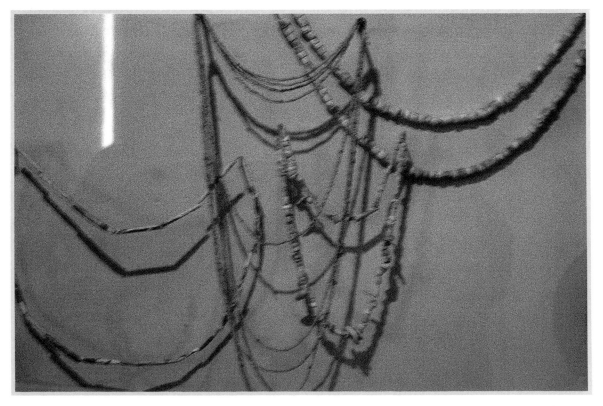

A wide variety of beads were used by the Esselen. These examples were recovered from Mission Carmel.

Villages

Most of the Esselen people's lives were spent in their small communities. Based on mission records, some modern scholars have suggested that there were villages known as Capanay, Ippimeguan, Jojopan, Ecgeagan, Eslanagan, Echilat, Hasshowwen, and Agua Caliente. Other researchers disagree. We will probably never know for sure how many villages and camps there were, or where they were located.

The Esselen communities probably varied in size. Among the Ohlones to the north, some settlements included as few as fifty people. The scarcity of resources in the Esselen homeland probably meant that the largest communities did not have more than two hundred people.

Like other California Native Americans, the Esselen selected sites for their settlements that were close to a supply of flowing water. The houses of the villages were probably laid out around an open space. Like other coastal California groups, the Esselen lived in small huts made out of poles, bark, grass, brush, ferns, bulrushes, or reeds. They called their homes *iwano*.

As with neighboring groups, each dwelling probably housed one or two related families. The dwellings had circular floor plans and ranged from 6 to 20 feet (2 to 6 m) in diameter. An opening was left in the middle of the roof. It allowed sunlight into the house, and made it possible for smoke to escape. When it rained, a piece of

16 This is a present-day photo of Sargenta-Ruc, also known as the Ranchería del Sur, in California. It was once the site of an important Esselen village.

animal skin was used to cover the hole. People slept on top of reed mats or blankets next to the walls. They usually dug a hearth, or fire pit, in the middle of the room. The fire heated the home and was used to prepare food. When the weather was good, most of the meals were cooked outside. The houses also sheltered each family's other property, including blankets, hunting equipment, fishing gear, and baskets.

Some of the Esselen settlements may have included a larger home that was reserved for the chief, or community leader. Similar structures were found among the Ohlones and some of the Esselen's relatives to the south. The extra space inside such homes was occupied by baskets filled with food. Sometimes the chief's house was used for special rituals and dances.

Also, the Esselen sometimes slept inside the caves and rock shelters that are found throughout their mountain homeland. One of these sites, called Isabella Meadows, produced evidence of people staying there off and on for several hundred years.

The Esselen may have also used small structures called granaries. These devices looked like baskets elevated above the ground by a large rock, or four strong poles. The granaries were filled with acorns, pine nuts, and other similar seeds. These items were eaten during the winter.

The Esselen villages almost certainly included sweat lodges. These structures were similar to houses except that they were partially buried in the ground. Inside of the cramped rooms, a fire produced intense heat and clouds of smoke. A small hole in the middle of the roof allowed the smoke to escape. The people had to crawl through a low doorway to get in and out of the structure. The sweat lodges were used for cleaning and healing. After they had been inside a sweat lodge for a while, people used curved sticks or deer ribs to scrape away their sweat.

The Esselen villages probably also included various kinds of pole-and-thatch coverings that provided shade. Men and women often sat in the shelter of these structures while they prepared food or made objects, such as stone tools.

When an Esselen person died, he or she may have been buried or cremated (burned) before burial. We do not know many details about where the remains were placed, but evidence shows that sometimes they were buried close to their villages, in community cemeteries.

Although each Esselen village may have had a well-known main location, it is likely that many of the people worked in other parts of their territory for long periods. Some scholars believe that the Esselen often relocated their settlements to take advantage of different kinds of resources. For example, when certain kinds of wild plants were ready to be harvested, they would move their settlements closer to the areas where the plants grew. Because their homes were easy to build, the frequent movement of the communities did not make too much extra work. Other researchers think that the Esselen had more permanent villages. They believe that people who were too old to work, or who were seriously ill, usually stayed at the main villages.

Cooking

Evidence from surrounding groups suggests that Esselen women used many different cooking techniques to create meals. Some of the wild foods that they depended on, such as acorns, had to be ground into powder and soaked in fresh water to remove poisonous substances. Some plants, such as wild berries and pine nuts, could be eaten with little or no preparation.

The Esselen probably used cooking methods that were similar to those used by their neighbors. These nations often cooked using an open flame. Other foods were prepared with steam, or they were smoked using slow-burning fires.

Most California Native Americans used pit ovens. These devices consisted of large holes that were dug into the ground. A fire was

Esselen artifacts are washing out of the black soil of midden, or a prehistoric trash heap. Fragments of shells that were thrown away during cooking are particularly abundant in the coastal sites. This midden was formed by people living in one place for several hundred years.

built in the center of the pit. Large stones were slowly added to the flames. When the rocks were red hot, poles or long sticks were used to drag them out of the pit. Some of the stones were put back into the hole, along with food, such as meat wrapped in leaves. The remaining heated rocks were piled on top. After a few hours, the meal would be ready to be served.

The Esselen prepared stews and similar hot dishes using tightly woven baskets. Stones that had been heated in a fire were placed into the mixtures. A person had to be careful to constantly stir the contents, or the stones would burn a hole in the baskets. Similar techniques were used to cook seeds and nuts.

Many of the Esselen's foods were only available during certain seasons. The people probably moved their homes to take advantage of the foods' abundance in different areas. Some things could be preserved for later use. The meat and fish that were brought to the village by hunters could be salted and smoked. Many of the plant foods could be dried in the sun.

Other Arts and Crafts

The few artifacts that have survived suggest that the Esselen produced remarkable artwork and crafts. The general characteristics of their work were probably similar to that of their neighbors, the Ohlones and the Salinans. Nearly all Native Americans depended on stone as one of their most important resources. The Esselen

This is a native traditional basket from Mission Carmel that may have been manufactured by Esselen craftspeople.

ground harder types of rocks into several different forms. Pestles, which are long stone cylinders, were used in combination with rocks that had large, round holes called mortars. Sometimes the Esselen used the massive boulders along the sides of creeks to create mortars. These hole-filled rocks were called bedrock mortars. All these devices were used to crack and grind acorns, pine nuts, and other seeds. Like other early Native Americans, the Esselen also created many types of chipped stone objects, including arrowheads, knives, and many similar cutting tools.

Scholars believe that, like their neighbors, the Esselen made many items from the creatures that they hunted. Skins were used to make blankets, skirts, quivers to hold arrows, and robes. Bones were transformed into beads, earrings, fishhooks, musical instruments, and many other tools. Bird feathers were used to make or decorate arrows, bows, capes, and dance skirts. Seashells became bowls, fishhooks, razors, and jewelry. The brains of some animals, such as deer, were used to tan hides.

Plants provided another important source of raw materials for all California Native Americans. Plants of many types, including grass and reeds, were collected and woven into baskets. Wood was used to make arrows, bows, digging sticks, and many other tools. Wood and basketry were combined to make other useful things, such as cradleboards for babies and fish traps. Other plants were used as medicines, poisons, and glue. Plant fibers were beaten, dried, and combined to create rope, nets, and cloth.

The Esselen probably used reed canoes, called *tule balsas*. These boats were made out of cigar-shaped bundles of rushes that were tied together. The vessels of their neighbors were about 10 feet long (about 3 m) and 3 feet wide (about 1 m). The boats could hold up to four people. They were used to fish and hunt in coastal waters and rivers. The *tule balsas'* crews used wooden paddles and stone anchors.

Iron and steel tools, such as the ones shown here from Mission Carmel, were provided to the Esselen during the early colonial period.

Three

Other Features of Esselen Life

Very little information has survived to help us understand Esselen language, social structure, government, warfare, and religion. Although they may have shared many traditions and customs with their neighbors, they probably also had many parts of their culture that were unique. Unfortunately, information about these parts of the Esselen story has been lost forever.

Language

The last person who spoke Esselen died in 1939. The language that she spoke was never completely recorded. Teams of scholars have studied lists of words and sentences. They classify the language as being part of the larger Hokan language family. Native Americans living to the south of the Esselen, including the Salinans and the Chumash, shared this language family. It is unclear how many different related language groups, or dialects, were spoken inside the Esselen country. Based on related groups living to the south of the Esselen, it seems likely that they could tell where another Esselen came from by how he or she spoke.

Much of the coastline of the Esselen area has dramatic cliffs and small rocky islands that are still the homes of sea birds, seals, and sea lions.

Social Structure

The smallest Ohlone social unit was the family. Most of the men had one wife. Wealthier villagers sometimes had two wives. The village chief was the only man allowed to have three wives. The work that each family member was assigned was usually determined by a person's age and gender. Ohlone families were combined into larger groups called clans. Clan members believed that their founding father was an animal, such as a bear, an eagle, or an antelope. Every clan had certain religious responsibilities. The clans were further grouped into two larger units, called moieties.

Some anthropologists that specialize in studying Native Americans believe that the combined Esselen communities probably formed a single tribelet, or political alliance. Other researchers feel that the region included five or six separate political groups who shared a common language and culture. It seems likely that all the people combined to form a single nation when outsiders, such as the Spaniards and the Ohlones, confronted them.

It is very likely that the men who led the Esselen villages were chiefs. Among other Native Americans in coastal California, this office was usually handed down from father to son. A council of village elders aided most chiefs. The chiefs were given special privileges. They collected gifts of all kinds from their people. However, most of the items were given back to the community during religious ceremonies, or they were used to entertain guests from other communities. The chief and council of elders provided overall leadership for most communities.

Throughout most of coastal California, both men and women could become spiritual leaders. These individuals were generally believed to have special abilities that could be used for both good and evil. The spiritual leaders knew many special rituals, dances, and songs, which were believed to have the power to make people well or sick. The Esselen also believed that their spiritual leaders controlled the weather. The spiritual leaders were always respected, and sometimes feared.

Magnificent eagles that inspired native legends still soar through the skies of the area where Esselen people made their villages.

Warfare

Fragmentary evidence suggests that warfare was an important activity for the Esselen. Their main weapons were the bow and the spear. The Esselen had a reputation for being particularly excellent archers. As in other parts of California, wars were fought for a variety of reasons. Sometimes they involved competition over natural resources, such as hunting-and-gathering areas. Other struggles developed out of accusations of witchcraft or other kinds of arguments. The Esselen's chief enemies were the Ohlones who lived just to the north, near Monterey and Carmel. The Esselen seem to have enjoyed more positive relations with the Salinan who lived to their south.

Throughout coastal California, most major conflicts involved raids. Groups of young warriors would invade enemy territory and capture or kill anyone they found. If they had a chance, the California Native Americans sometimes destroyed whole villages. However, the wars usually ended when the chiefs of the two groups worked out an agreement.

Some California Native Americans also engaged in a kind of ritualized warfare to resolve disputes. Both sides would meet at a certain place and time. Speakers urged the men to show bravery with dances, songs, and similar rituals. Eventually, one or two warriors were killed. Afterward, one side or the other would retreat and ask for peace.

Religion

Like other native peoples, the Esselen probably had many beliefs and stories about how their world came into being. Most Native Americans' lives were filled with rituals that marked the journey a person makes from birth to death, as well as events such as the changing seasons. There must have been many elaborate holidays and celebrations. The seasons of the year were kept track of by the movement of the stars and their closeness to the yearly harvests. People often sought out spirit helpers that are associated with animals, such as wolves and mountain lions. One Spaniard said that the natives believed that when they died, their spirits became owls.

This picture was created around 1792 by a Spanish artist. It shows the clothing and appearance of natives from the Monterey area. The individuals are either Esselen or their close neighbors, the southern Ohlone. Both groups wore similar clothing.

Nearly all of California's Native Americans worshiped through songs and dance. They probably used musical instruments similar to those of the Ohlones, such as flutes, rattles, and whistles. Most coastal Native Americans used split pieces of wood called clapper sticks to beat out a rhythm.

Like their Salinan relatives to the south, the Esselen often marked the surface of cave walls and rocks with symbols. This kind of work is called rock art. Some were made using paint. These pictures are called pictographs. Other marks were made by pecking away some of the rocks' surface. This kind of picture is called a petroglyph. We do not know exactly why the Esselen made rock art. Most people believe that the pictures were created as part of their religion. Because rock art is sacred to many modern Native Americans, it is very important that people show respect when they view it.

The rock art of the Esselen included mysterious depictions of human hands. No one knows the exact meaning of these and other similar native symbols.

Four

The Esselen and the Newcomers

In 1602 Sebastian Vizcaíno became the first European to explore the general region occupied by the Esselen. During his examination of the Monterey Bay area, he probably met with some of these Native Americans who lived in the nearby mountains. Vizcaíno's trip to California was undertaken to locate a harbor where the Spanish ships traveling to the Philippines could stop and rest. Vizcaíno was so impressed by Monterey Bay that he told the king of Spain that it would make an excellent site for a colony. However, a series of delays prevented the Spanish government from building an outpost in California for more than one hundred and fifty years.

Between 1602 and 1769, many other explorers and Spanish merchant ships stopped on the California coast. We do not have any detailed descriptions about the events that took place among the Native Americans of California during this period. Evidence from other regions suggests that throughout most of the New World, newcomers from Europe introduced terrifying diseases that may have killed as many as ninety-five percent of the native population. Given the frequent visits of Spaniards to California, it is likely that most coastal groups, including the Esselen, suffered terrible losses. By the time the Spaniards came to

This is a depiction of a Spanish soldier attacking Indians from the Monterey area. The natives shown may be Esselen or Ohlone. This picture was created about 1792 by the Spanish artist José Cardero.

stay in Monterey in 1770, the population had probably gone down, and then increased, as it had with most Native Americans.

The Esselen and the Spaniards

By 1750, King Carlos III of Spain had become fearful of English and Russian expeditions that were exploring the Pacific Ocean. He realized that if California was taken over by one of his European rivals, the excellent port of Monterey could be used to launch invasions of Mexico and Peru. These two kingdoms were the richest parts of his empire. In desperation, he ordered his officials to figure out a way for Spain to gain control of upper California. In 1769, an expedition was launched to make the region a province of the Spanish Empire. The next year, the capital of the new territory was established on Monterey. This outpost included a military base and a mission. The army was sent to block foreigners from entering the region.

King Carlos III wanted to take over California. However, he did not have the colonists, money, or soldiers needed to conquer the region. The king's officials decided that their only hope was to build a bond of friendship with some of the Native Americans. They decided that missions would be used to expand Spain's hold on the remote province. These missions would be built as religious communities where Native Americans would gradually be transformed into Spanish citizens. The crown officials selected a group of Franciscan priests, headed by Junípero Serra, to lead this project.

The Franciscans who were selected were eager to go to California as missionaries. From their point of view, their efforts would provide them with an opportunity to share their religion and to help poor people. The priests were also happy to serve their government. They believed that they could build mission communities that combined the best characteristics of the European and Native American worlds. The Franciscans were certain that Europe had many things that could improve the lives of Native Americans: advanced technology, medicine, science, and engineering. They also believed that European plants, such as wheat, and animals, such as cattle and horses, could make the Native Americans' lives easier. The Franciscans also expected to gain Native American knowledge that could improve their own lives and those of other Europeans. Their overall goal was to build a religious community that would improve the futures of both Spaniards and the Native Americans.

The Esselen and the Beginnings of Mission San Carlos Borromeo

In contrast with many of the coastal peoples of California, the Esselen were only involved with a single mission, Mission San Carlos Borromeo. Like the other settlements established by the Franciscans, Mission San Carlos Borromeo was much more than a church where natives learned about Christianity. Each of these settlements was also an outpost of empire that was a kind of government agency. Here, Native

Americans were introduced to many aspects of the Spanish way of life, including a whole range of new ideas, animals, plants, and tools.

In order for the Franciscans to be able to build the missions, they had to persuade the Esselen to join the new communities. Why would any Native American want to live in a mission? Moving to one of the Franciscan settlements offered a number of practical benefits. At the start of the missions, the priests almost always offered the native people gifts of food, cloth, and other small items, such as trade beads. Once the Native Americans were close enough to really see the newcomers, they could not help noticing other advantages in having them as friends. The Spaniards had powerful weapons, such as ships, firearms, and steel swords. They would make good allies during any war. The foreigners also brought steel axes, knives, dozens of new kinds of food, and animals, such as horses, sheep, cattle, mules, and chickens. The Franciscan priests also had many things of beauty, including paintings, statues, religious rituals, and powerful music. The newcomers promised the Esselen friendship, help during times of war, and opportunities to gain access to the new materials if they stayed and lived at the missions.

The Esselen were probably also persuaded to come to live at the mission by the speeches that they heard from the priests. Junípero Serra undertook much of the early work with the Native Americans who moved to Mission San Carlos. This man had a reputation for giving powerful, dramatic speeches. Both European and native audiences often became emotional as the small man with a large dream spoke about what he believed could be their future. Throughout coastal California, he persuaded natives and colonists to join with him in his goal of creating a new kind of utopia, or perfect world. Although his vision was never achieved, many people who lived in California between 1769 and 1835 found themselves working together to try to create communities that were as close to heaven on Earth as they could. It is impossible to say how many of the native people were attracted to the Franciscans' ideals. However, according to Spanish observers, most of the Esselen quickly moved to the mission. Once they resettled there, they showed few signs of having regretted their choice to start a new way of life.

If the Native Americans had chosen not to move into the mission, there was very little that the government could have done to force them to live there. The vast, rugged mountains of the Esselen homeland provided thousands of hiding places. As small as the Esselen Nation was, it still outnumbered the force of fifty men who protected the nearby military base at Monterey. If they had chosen to, the Esselen could have made the creation of Mission San Carlos impossible.

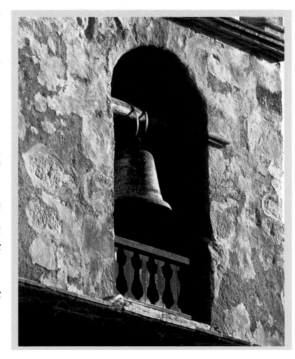

Bells still call people to prayer at Mission Carmel.

At first, it looked as if this might take place. Between 1771 and 1773, close contacts between the Esselen and the newcomers were almost always less than friendly. Fortunately for both groups, no one was killed or seriously hurt in these confrontations.

Why were the Esselen hostile to the priests and soldiers, while the local Ohlones seemed friendly? When they created Mission San Carlos in June of 1770, the newcomers had unknowingly formed an alliance with Ohlone people who were the Esselen's traditional enemies. It took a while for the Spaniards to understand this situation. When they did, they realized they could use the conflict between natives to their advantage by seeking alliances with both groups. Thus, the Esselen choice to live at the mission may have also been encouraged by their fear that their Ohlone enemies might use their influence to get the newcomers to attack and destroy them. As in so many parts of America, the divisions between natives served as a source of European power. Before 1775, the Franciscans had negotiated a peace between the two warring parties, and proved to the Esselen's satisfaction that they too were welcome to live at the mission as friends. The peace established by Serra persisted throughout the years that followed.

The Franciscans called the Esselen who decided to move to the missions neophytes, or new followers. Based on what happened at other missions, it seems likely that the native chiefs brought their communities to the new settlements. Once they had moved, the

Esselen elders often continued to serve as leaders. The neophytes were allowed to visit and trade with non-Christian Native Americans who lived in the interior. They sometimes persuaded their relatives, who the Spaniards called gentiles, to come and live with them.

At first, not all the Esselen decided to join the mission. Before 1814, at least a few of them deserted to the mountains, where they lived a lifestyle based on capturing mission cattle, sheep, and horses. Elsewhere in California, greater numbers of people who moved into the missions decided to run away. Other natives tried to keep their distance from the newcomers. Some of the Esselen may have managed to live in remote places in their mountains and continue most, if not all, of their ancient customs.

The first mission complex consisted of a small wooden fort, which contained a church and a home for the priests and a few soldiers. Outside the wooden walls was a large village of native homes. Within the neophyte settlement, there were two distinct sections. One was lived in by the Ohlones. The Esselen lived in the second part of the village. For many years, there was probably some level of tension between these two groups. These feelings probably disappeared as the two nations got to know each other, and realized that differences between people did not mean that they had to hate each other. Life at Mission San Carlos soon provided many new experiences for the neophytes. The Franciscans quickly introduced European technologies and ideas to the natives. Soon Mission San Carlos began to change and grow.

Mission Success and Failure

By 1780, a new complex of adobe, or earth block, structures with grass roofs served as a church, offices, workshops, and homes for the newcomers. The population of the Ohlones and Esselen villages continued to grow as more and more native groups decided that their best hope for the future was to move to Mission San Carlos. Marriages between the two groups became more common. The neophytes quickly learned many European trades and customs. The Franciscans ran Mission San Carlos with the help of Native American leaders.

This sketch depicts a French visitor greeting the native people at Mission Carmel in 1786.

For many years, the missionaries did not try to change the natives' way of life, except where the natives' beliefs were in direct conflict with what the missionaries believed were important religious ideas. Some natives resented the priests' beliefs about marriages and personal freedom. However, whatever hard feelings came up, they did not lead to any major trouble at Mission San Carlos.

By the end of the century, the mission was enjoying its greatest period of prosperity and success. By 1810, the settlement had developed into an all-adobe-and-tile complex. The magnificent stone church that still stands was the product of native laborers and craftsmen who worked under the direction of the architect, Manuel Estevan Ruíz. Nearly all the major buildings had red tile roofs and white plastered walls. For many years, the neophytes continued to prefer to live in their traditional styles of homes. A few foreign visitors to Mission San Carlos noted that these structures provided little protection to their inhabitants. During the early part of the new century the neophytes moved into adobe homes that were similar to those used at the nearby settlement of Monterey.

A visitor to the mission could easily see the progress. The neophytes performed Spanish music with their own orchestras and sang religious songs in Latin, Ohlone, and Esselen. The mission had aqueducts, dams, fountains, orchards, warehouses, and factories, which turned out blankets, clothing, and furniture. The Native Americans learned to wear some European-style clothing and had household tools that were identical to the ones found among the Spanish colonists.

Many neophyte families ground their acorns, wheat, and corn using the newcomers' style of stone tools instead of their own mortars and pestles. They roasted food and baked bread in Spanish-style adobe ovens. Small adobe-and-tile stoves had replaced the older types of cooking hearths. Metal or pottery bowls and pots replaced many of the older styles of baskets. Steel knives and similar metal tools could be found in every house.

The neophytes also served as expert farmers and cowboys. Mission San Carlos owned thousands of head of cattle and grew enough food to support a much larger population. Some of the mission's ranches and farms were built inside the old Esselen territory. However, experiments with plants and animals taught the missionaries that much of the Esselen homeland was too rugged, and too cold, for the kinds of plants and animals that they depended on. Although most of the lands that produced food were located outside of the old Esselen territory, everyone who lived at the outpost shared in the products and the harvests. The hard work of the native people made all the accomplishments of the mission possible.

A visitor to Mission San Carlos would have also seen that a great deal of time was set aside for fun. The community celebrated more holidays than we enjoy today. After the end of the workday, neophytes followed many of their traditional kinds of recreation. There were dances, races, gambling, and a great deal of socializing. For several weeks out of the year, the neophytes made extended trips into their old homeland to fish, hunt, hold celebrations, and gather traditional foods. Spanish priests and soldiers took no part in these journeys, which some scholars have described as vacations.

As the mission grew, contact with the Spanish and Mexican colonists at the nearby military town of Monterey gradually increased. By 1800, the neophytes frequently traded with, or worked in their spare time for, the settlers. They also joined together with the colonists at larger religious ceremonies and various government celebrations. The newcomers respected the natives' honesty and their skills. The missionaries accepted the neophytes' visits to the settlers in part because they helped to promote the natives' adoption of Spanish customs. The neophytes also learned many of the colonists' less admirable customs. They soon adopted Spanish drinking practices, as well as the newcomers' love of gambling on card games and horse races.

Besides adopting many European customs, the Esselen people also accepted many traditions of the Ohlones who also lived at the mission. As marriages between the two groups increased, their cultures were slowly combined. Most of the children of mixed families spoke Ohlone or Spanish instead of Esselen. The reasons for this choice are unclear. However, Ohlone and Spanish may have been more useful because more people outside the mission spoke these languages. In any event, after 1814, the Esselen language began to be spoken less frequently.

From the outside, it seemed that all the neophytes had learned to live and think like Europeans. Evidence from other mission communities suggests that appearances often hid another reality. Even the most willing neophytes did not completely forget their traditional customs. The natives usually mastered the new ways, but preserved what they considered to be the best of their older traditions, including their ideas about the world and their stories.

A visitor to the mission in 1810 was also unlikely to have realized that dark forces were already at work that would prevent the bright future for the neophytes that had been dreamed of by Father Serra and many natives. While there was obvious evidence of prosperity, European diseases were taking a terrible toll. The simple truth is that more people died each year than were born. In 1795, Mission San Carlos had almost nine hundred neophytes. During the next fifteen years, the supply of new converts dried up. No one realized it at the time, but the mission was already doomed.

Disease and the Decline of the Mission

After 1800, the Franciscans realized that something had to be changed, or the population of Mission San Carlos would eventually disappear. Between 1795 and 1822, the settlement suffered a loss of nearly two-thirds of its people. The Franciscans could not understand what was going wrong. More often than not, they blamed the close contact with soldiers and settlers for spreading diseases among their followers. They probably did not realize it, but the priests also brought many new sicknesses to the natives. It was clear that the neophytes died from many of the same illnesses that the Europeans easily survived.

The Franciscans tried to use every method they had to stop the spread of disease. However, the medicines and treatments that both the natives and the priests knew about often did more harm than good. For example, the Franciscans often gave milk to the people who were sick. Among Europeans, milk was thought to be one of the best sources of nourishment that a sick person could drink. Unfortunately, milk makes most Native American people sick. By having the neophytes who were ill drink milk, the Franciscans actually made most of them sicker. The new diseases also devastated many Native Americans who lived close to the frontier, outside of the missions. It is also clear that some native groups survived more

successfully than others. Perhaps the centuries of isolation in the remote mountains had made the Esselen more vulnerable to the newcomers' sicknesses.

The problems faced by the priests at Mission San Carlos were not unique. Many other Franciscan settlements were only able to grow by constantly increasing their population

This is the reconstructed communal kitchen from Mission Carmel. Native cooks prepared meals for the priests in kitchens similar to this one.

with new converts. Unlike other missions, no effort was made to bring additional native groups to the settlement. Why did the Franciscans choose not to bring converts from more distant areas to Mission San Carlos? Although the lands of the settlement could easily support its shrinking population, the priests of Mission San Carlos did not have the supply of rich agricultural and ranch lands needed to support additional growth. The nearby town of Monterey was filled with colonists who tried to occupy the best mission lands. In short, even if the population had been growing, it was evident that the future was less than bright for the Franciscan outpost. In 1803, the priests recognized the limited future of San Carlos when the new Franciscan leader moved his headquarters to the thriving Chumash mission settlement at Santa Bárbara. Given the decades of shrinking population, it was clear in 1821 that Mission San Carlos would soon become a ghost town.

The End of the Mission Period

Changes in government policy ended the story of Mission San Carlos before it had lost all of its population. Although the community had far fewer people than it did in 1795, the mission experienced a kind of prosperity during its final years that could still impress foreign visitors. The wealth seen at San Carlos, and other Franciscan outposts, was mostly based on profits that were made through trade with foreign merchants.

The first serious signs of future trouble with government officials appeared during the Mexican War of Independence (1810-1821). After 1810, the Spanish frontier army and settlers borrowed huge amounts of money, supplies, and workers from the Franciscan settlements. Mission San Carlos even had to provide temporary barracks for troops. The priests expected to be paid for these goods and services at the end of the conflict.

In 1822, the shocking news arrived that the year before, the Spanish army had surrendered California. The people of Mission San Carlos were now part of the new nation of Mexico. The missionaries soon learned that they were not to receive any payment for the support that they had given to the frontier army and the Spanish government. When they asked who was going to pay them for all their

This is Mission Carmel in 1826 as shown in a painting by a visiting English artist. The native housing was located to the right of the church.

goods and services, they were told to take their demands to the King of Spain. The local settlers, many of whom had gone without pay for more than a decade, also refused to pay their debts.

Not all the news was so grim for the neophytes. Some political leaders from the new government promised them that they would soon be given complete control of the mission towns and other property. The native leaders were anxious to take their place in the new society of Mexico. However, the promises of freedom and civil rights would never be completely fulfilled. Delay followed delay as church officials, the army, and the government in Mexico City argued about the wisdom of ending the Franciscans' role at the missions.

In 1827, a new law made it possible for some of the neophytes to find a future outside of the Franciscan community. Twenty-three men legally departed the settlement with their priests' blessings to become regular Mexican citizens. They were given small plots of land and tools to live as farmers. Without any clear means of making a living, most of the natives soon found work at local ranches and in the nearby military town of Monterey. Between 1829 and 1831, another forty people decided to leave the mission and take up life in the newcomers' communities.

By 1831, it was clear that time was running out for Mission San Carlos. During the last ten years, the population had dropped by nearly another third, to 229 people. About half of those who stayed at the mission were now too old to work.

The community barely produced enough food to meet its needs. When the end finally came in 1834, the government was supposed to give the Native American leaders, including those of Mission San Carlos, the control of their lands and other property. If this had taken place, the surviving 185 neophytes would have become some of the richest people in California. Instead, a few greedy Mexican settlers took almost everything of value that the Native Americans possessed. These newcomers took all the best farmland and ranching country.

The Esselen After the Mission Experience

After 1834, the former natives of Mission San Carlos faced a world of limited choices. Some became cowboys and servants. Others were forced by powerful landowners to work without pay. Much of the old territory between Mission San Antonio and Mission San Carlos remained unoccupied. However, during the previous sixty years, horses, sheep, and cattle had changed even the most remote places. These animals ate traditional crops and disrupted nearly all aspects of the natural environment. By 1834, the old Esselen way of living could not easily be recreated. Besides, the Esselen people who had lived at the mission had grown used to their new way of life. A few natives probably returned to their old lands. Some families from the Monterey area remember stories that tell about a small group of

49

Esselen who had lived in the mountains but moved into the new-comers' settlements about 1840.

Throughout California, many former neophytes escaped east-ward and joined with other independent Native American nations. They helped to organize raiding parties that captured thousands of head of cattle and horses from the Mexican ranches. By 1845, it looked as if the Native Americans might drive the newcomers out of California.

Everything changed dramatically after the Mexican-American War. The treaty of 1848, which ended the conflict, made California a part of the United States. The former neophytes quickly discovered that the new government was less friendly than the previous ones. The U.S. Army quickly crushed any Native American resistance. The Gold Rush of 1849 brought tens of thousands of new people from all over the world. The remaining open lands that had once belonged to Native Americans in the areas around the missions were quickly occupied without any regard to earlier claims of ownership.

The United States government denied nearly all Native Americans their basic rights as human beings. By 1900, most of the remaining people whose ancestors had lived at the missions realized that as long as they said that they were Indians, they would be stripped of nearly all their rights. Many Native Americans told the government officials that they were Mexicans. Although these people were not treated fairly by the state or the federal government, they were not treated as badly as were Native Americans. The mission survivors were accepted by many poor people who were Mexicans because many of them also had Native American ancestors.

This painting shows the prosperity found in the new mining areas during the California Gold Rush.

Five

The Esselen Heritage

The story of the Esselen after 1770 is one of tragedy. No doubt, they never expected or wanted to disappear as a people. One can only imagine how sad the Franciscans who came to help them would be if they could see what happened after 1800. The Esselen's mountain way of life was probably one of the first California native cultures to disappear as a result of the European invasion.

Evidence, gathered largely from Spanish accounts, suggests that these Native Americans enthusiastically joined the missions and were incorporated into the Spanish world. They appear to have accepted their new lives, despite the terrible losses to European diseases. The descendants of the early Esselen survived as part of a new kind of community that incorporated their customs and traditions with those of the Ohlone people who shared the mission. As time progressed, the surviving Esselen customs and language became less and less important to their descendants. The horrors that followed the end of the mission period in 1834 further washed away whatever remained of the Esselen way of life.

During the early twentieth century, anthropologists began serious studies of California's Native Americans. By the time that scholars were trying to get information from Native Americans about their culture, people who spoke the Esselen language or

Esselen art and artifacts are very scarce. However, the Esselen presence can still be felt at some sacred sites.

who even identified themselves as Esselen could not be found. Costanoans, or Ohlones, from the Monterey area provided researchers with small amounts of information about the group.

A few of the objects produced by the Esselen have been excavated from archaeological sites. Most of these objects can be found among museum collections in universities in California. Almost no obvious evidence can be seen of the Esselen presence in the region that was once their homeland. Beyond the modern communities of Monterey and Carmel, there are vast stretches of still-rugged mountains protected as part of the Ventana Wilderness Area of Los Padres National Forest. If you know where to look, you can still find some of the Esselen sacred places and home sites. Mission San Carlos Borromeo still stands, but it offers few displays that focus on the Native Americans who lived there.

Today, small communities of Esselen descendants are seeking to revive portions of their lost ways. It is a difficult struggle. Some of these individuals can be found in the Ohlone/Costanoan Esselen Nation of Monterey County. No one knows how many descendants exist. They live as part of the larger American population and do not have any kind of reservation. They are not even recognized as Native Americans by the U.S. government.

There is no doubt that the ancient Esselen people had many things of great value that have been lost forever. The end of their customs and language are a tragedy, not just for their descendants, but also for everyone. We will never know what truths the Esselen may have discovered. When any culture disappears, its loss makes every human's life a little poorer. Far too many native cultures in the Americas disappeared when the Old World encountered the new. We need to treat what remains of the Esselen heritage with a special kind of respect and an understanding that we all need to work to prevent the disappearance of other small cultures. We owe it to ourselves, and the memory of the Esselen.

Timeline

Between 13,000–40,000 years ago	The ancestors of the Esselen arrive in North America from Asia.
By 8,000 years ago	People settle along the coastline of California. Some of these groups were probably relatives of the Esselen.
1602	Sebastian Vizcaíno visits Monterey Bay, close to the Esselen area, and claims it for Spain.
1769	The first Spanish colonists invade California.
1770–1771	A military base and a mission is established just to the north of the Esselen territory at Monterey. The mission is soon moved to the Carmel River. In 1771, a second mission is established just to the south of the Esselen country among the Salinans, at San Antonio.
By 1775	Large numbers of Esselen people become neophytes.

1795	Mission San Carlos has over nine hundred native Esselen and Ohlone residents. The population will soon begin to decline as a result of European introduced diseases.
1821	Mexico becomes independent of Spain. The Esselen become citizens of the new nation.
1827–1832	Small numbers of Esselen and Ohlones leave Mission San Carlos to become farmers and laborers.
1833–1835	The missions of California are eliminated by the order of the Mexican government.
1848	The Mexican-American War ends, and the United States takes control of California. Native Americans lose their status as citizens.
1850–1900	Numerous laws are passed that deny Native Americans their basic human rights.
1924	All Native Americans are made United States citizens.
1975– present	Some Esselen descendants become involved in the Native American civil rights movement.

Glossary and Pronunciation Guide

adobe (uh-DOH-bee)   A kind of brick made from mud and straw.

anthropologist (an-thruh-POL-uh-jist)   Scholars who study all aspects of what it means to be human.

artifacts (AR-tee-fakts)   Any object showing evidence of human activity.

aqueduct (AK-wuh-duhkt)   A man-made channel used to carry water.

bedrock mortar (BED-rok MOR-tur)   A kind of rock face with holes that were used to grind seed and nuts into flour.

chief (CHEEF)   A kind of leader who receives special privileges and redistributes goods that he collects to his people.

clans (KLANZ)   A group of families that claim to be related to the same animal ancestor.

clapper sticks (KLAP-puhr STIKS)   A kind of musical instrument that was used to beat out rhythm.

culture (KUHL-chur)   Shared, learned behavior.

descendants (dih-SEN-dents)   People who can trace their ancestors to a particular person.

gentile (JEN-tile)   A word used for non-Christian Native Americans under Spanish rule.

hearth (HARTH) A pit used for fires.

iwano (EE-whan-oo) An Esselen word meaning house.

middens (MID-denz) Trash piles.

mission (MISH-uhn) In colonial California, a kind of Spanish settlement where Native Americans were to be transformed into Christian citizens.

moiety (MOY-ay-tee) A kind of social unit that divides a community into two groups, based on family relationships.

mortars (MOR-turz) Circular holes in rocks that were used to crack nuts and grind seeds into flour.

neophytes (NEE-oh-fites) A term used for mission Indians who were new followers of the Christian religion.

pestles (PESS-tuhlz) Cylindrical-shaped pieces of rocks used with mortars.

social structure (SOH-shul STRUHK-chur) A way of dividing a community into different groups of people.

tribelet (TRIBE-let) A term sometimes used by anthropologists for what the Ohlones considered to be their nations.

tule balsa (TOO-lee BALL-saw) A kind of canoe made from bundles of reeds.

utopia (YOU-toe-pee-ah) A kind of ideal community where everyone is treated fairly and is happy.

Resources

BOOKS

Campbell, Paul. *Survival Skills of Native California.* Salt Lake City, UT: Gibbs Smith, 1999.

Malinowski, Sharon (editor). *Gale Encyclopedia of Native American Tribes* (volume three). Detroit, MI: Gale Group, 1998.

Margolin, Malcolm. *The Ohlone Way Indian Life in the San Francisco-Monterey Bay Area.* Berkeley, CA: Heyday Books, 1981.

Milliken, Randall. *A Time of Little Choice: The Disintegration of Tribal Culture in the San Francisco Bay Area, 1769–1810.* Menlo Park, CA: Ballena Press, 1995.

Williams, Jack S. *The Ohlone of California.* New York: Rosen Publishing Group, 2003.

MISSIONS, MUSEUMS, AND PARKS

Mission San Antonio de Padua

P.O. Box 803

Mission Creek Road

Jolon, CA 93928

Web site: http://www.missionsanantoniopadua.com

Mission San Carlos Borromeo de Carmelo

3080 Rio Road

Carmel, CA 93923

(831) 624-3600

Web site: http://www.carmelmission.org

Monterey County Historical Society

P.O. Box 3576

Salinas, CA 93912

(831) 757-8085

e-mail: mchs@dedot.com

Web site: http://users.dedot.com/mchs/index.html

Pfeiffer Big Sur State Park

47225 Highway 1

Big Sur, CA 93920

(831) 667-2315

WEB SITES

Due to the changing nature of Internet links, PowerKids Press has developed an online list of Web sites related to the subject of this book. This site is updated regularly. Please use this link to access the site:

www.powerkidslinks.com/lna/esselen

Index